Near and Far with Birds

By **Tyrone Mineo**

Gareth Stevens
Publishing

Please visit our website, www.garethstevens.com. For a free color catalog of all our high-quality books, call toll free 1-800-542-2595 or fax 1-877-542-2596.

Library of Congress Cataloging-in-Publication Data

Mineo, Tyrone.
Near and far with birds / Tyrone Mineo.
    p. cm. — (Animal math)
Includes index.
ISBN 978-1-4339-5668-3 (pbk.)
ISBN 978-1-4339-5669-0 (6-pack)
ISBN 978-1-4339-5666-9 (lib. bdg.)
1. Space perception—Juvenile literature. I. Title.
BF469.M5625 2011
153.7'52—dc22

                                    2010049269

First Edition

Published in 2012 by
Gareth Stevens Publishing
111 East 14th Street, Suite 349
New York, NY 10003

Designer: Haley W. Harasymiw
Editor: Therese M. Shea

Photo credits: Cover, pp. 1, 5, 7, 9, 11, 13, 15, 16, 17, 18, 19, 20, 21 Shutterstock.com.

Printed in the United States of America

CPSIA compliance information: Batch #CS11GS: For further information contact Gareth Stevens, New York, New York at 1-800-542-2595.

Contents

Boldface words appear in the glossary.

Ducks

Ducks love water. Their **webbed** feet help them swim.

This duck is near.

5

Some ducks fly to warm places in winter.

These ducks are far.

7

Parrots

These parrots are called lovebirds.

They like to be close.

These lovebirds are near each other.

These parrots are called macaws.
They have bright colors and
long tails.

These macaws are far from
each other.

Eagles

Eagles are large birds. They catch animals with their long **claws**.

Is this eagle near or far?

The bald eagle has a white head and tail. It is a **symbol** of the United States.

Is this bald eagle near or far?

Amazing Birds

Peregrine falcons are the fastest birds in the world.

Which falcon is farther away?

Ostriches are the biggest birds.

They cannot fly.

Which ostriches
are nearer?

Hummingbirds are the smallest birds. They get food from flowers.

Which hummingbird is nearer to the flowers?

21

Glossary

claw: an animal's sharp nail

symbol: something that stands for something else

webbed: joined by skin

Answer Key

page 12: near

page 14: far

page 16: falcon on page 17

page 18: ostriches on page 18

page 20: hummingbird on page 20

For More Information

Books

Johnson, Tami. *Near and Far.* Mankato, MN: Capstone Press, 2007.

Salzmann, Mary Elizabeth. *Brilliant Birds.* Edina, MN: ABDO Publishing, 2007.

Websites

Birds

nationalzoo.si.edu/Animals/Birds/ForKids/
Read about different kinds of birds and their lives.

A Game of Opposites

www.meddybemps.com/Opposites/
Learn about near and far as well as other opposites by playing a game.

Index